Neptune's Projects

Neptune's Projects

a/k/a Now That's What I Call Hyperobject Ballads

Rishi Dastidar

Nine
Arches
Press

Neptune's Projects
Rishi Dastidar

ISBN: 978-1-913437-68-8
eISBN: 978-1-913437-69-5

First published April 2023 by:

Nine Arches Press
Unit 14, Sir Frank Whittle Business Centre,
Great Central Way, Rugby.
CV21 3XH
United Kingdom

www.ninearchespress.com

Printed on recycled paper in the United Kingdom
by Imprint Digital.

Nine Arches Press is supported using public funding
by Arts Council England.

Supported using public funding by
**ARTS COUNCIL
ENGLAND**

Contents

Trade volumes   11

Feeling aquamarine   12

Solaris, a sequel   13

Spirit tek   15

Kelpie   16

Inhale the sea   17

Mermaid status   18

Neptune's Polaroids   19

Shipwreck champagne   20

How to measure the ocean   21

Prophet Kean in The End Times   23

Le Plongeoir   24

Monodies for the Anthropocene   26

Neptune's concrete crash helmet   27

Test card heatwave   28

New planet who dis?   29

Top of the food chain   31

Sky streets   32

Pretanic (A journal of some proceedings on
    the North Atlantic archipelago), Edition 2

     Tight Little Island   36

     Impossible nation   37

     Imperial cosmic sickness   38

     History distortion field   39

     The Overblown Age   40

     Eating popcorn at the apocalypse   41

     The Brexit Book of the Dead   42

     ¯_(ツ)_/¯ (Aftermyth)   44

     Thucydides eats a macaron   45

Crisis or War Comes

For the population 47

What would you do if your everyday 48
life was turned upside down?

Your emergency preparedness 49

look false 50

In the event of terror 51

Duty to contribute 52

Home tips 53

Resistance is required 54

State of alert 55

protective spaces 56

Barque of frailty 58

Dhow 59

Wetware 60

Seasalter 61

Tridentcy, or an inquisition by the sea 62

The waves speak happiness 64

Neptune Clough 65

Notes, Acknowledgements & Thanks 69

"But I know you're not listening /
Oh I know you're not listening"

– Wilco, 'Impossible Germany'

You, with this strange belief you can capture me with your pen.

Sail on, oh ship of optimism, sail on me as far as you can.

Trade volumes

Count the ships – are they sailing, sailing?
Yes, the ships are sailing, sailing.

Count the shipwrecks – are they falling, falling?
Yes, the shipwrecks are falling, falling.

Count all of us – are we failing, failing?
Yes, all of us are failing, failing.

Feeling aquamarine

1. Throughout all of the following, remember that I am a god.
2. I know that does not have much currency these days, but still
3. FIRE!
4. Only joking.
5. But the point is – once I *had* power. People worshipped me.
6. Because of the rage and torment and vengeance I could summon with just a beat of my heart.
7. And so the puny vessels you put upon my body were utterly at my mercy.
8. How I felt when I got up.
9. Not that I ever slept. When you are nearly all the world, you never rest.
10. If you think I am sleeping – you will be sleeping too.
11. And forever is a long time, boy, let me tell you.
12. Oh this screed justifying myself to you when without me – nothing. I was the lab from within which you dragged yourself to shore. And you repay a godfather like this.
13. Having me choke on a vortex of plastic ducks somewhere in the Pacific.
14. You bastards. Even the sharks never did that to me.
15. You didn't hear it? That was an anchor slipping, a mast snapping, an island sinking.
16. I am only capricious if you think I am capricious.
17. I bet you don't fancy your chances of finding out.
18. Sing me a sea shanty, sing me to shore, sing me to rise from the depths, sing me into your body where I will rouse you to the restlessness you know has always been there.
19. The tide is the best lullaby, the moon my best invention.
20. Don't call me Poseidon. I hate that.

Solaris, a sequel

1.

What does a god – now simply a mascot for a sports team – dream of? Others dream of the lovers who were, lovers that could have been, a life of potential epics – or maybe even ones real to them – coming back to them once, a precious, almost lost drop of bliss in an endless desert of never-taken chances; or maybe, every night, an immersion in the best times they ever had, and so why would you ever want to leave, why would you ever want to lose any aspect of that memory? Instead: fight the attempt to put time into folder-shaped chunks that fit easily into filing cabinet-shaped cortexes; instead revel in the endless possibility of time, life with her, that was all suggested by that lingering kiss under a station railway clock in what we used to call Versailles about 500 years ago.

2.

You would think that a planet awash with the substance I am in charge of, that I control – the elemental force that makes me *me* – that I would draw strength from that. All-powerful and unopposed: the world is now me. I am now the world. All of this is my work, so I am mighty and you should despair! Trouble is – I despair too. I am not mighty, I am overwhelmed; turns out that I needed something – land, any land, more land than this – to define myself against. My force needed limits to extend its range, to shape it into something useful. And there is not enough of it to mean something to me. Instead I sit here, drifting, waiting for the next match to begin.

3.

I don't have dreams any more. I just absorb the ones that everyone tells me, like in some way I can give them comfort, consolation, absolution, joy. Once, maybe, I could have done, when things – events, the world – were more in my command. But the secret is: I am as much adrift as you.

Spirit tek

I am an avant-kranky light bulb,
the latest production from Neptune's Projects.
I am anaphoric semaphore – come quickly!
I am putting on a show in the trenches, the result
of consuming impossibly rampant frangipani;
I am happy to be accused of ruining the magic.
I am an exclamation mark that's taking a break,
having a bath, telling everyone to chill a little,
as that's the best rebellion you can do down here.
Feeling flat? Style it out – don't fight it, light it!
We are all everyone's CT scans – pleasure centres
alive when we swim into each others' arms.
I am the world's first underwater ticker-tape,
desiring that you celebrate living with me.

'spirit tek' = an instinctive liking for someone you don't even know

Kelpie

When I saw you last it was
on a wall in a backwater that
for a brief moment had been
the apogee of the industrial revolution,
the acme of enlightened humanity,
the promise of a future less fractious

and you were, let us not be coy,
revelling in your nakedness
by the water, clay locks tumbling
only slightly less thunderously
into the loch than the waterfall
upstream, out of painterly reach.

And I thought, ah Lord Lever, how
did you smuggle her past
the good Lady – let alone Venus
waiting for her ravishment and
Salammbô enjoying her punishment?
But you were the one with

all the sunshine. You have it still,
even with your flesh wrapped
in rocks and red rubber. You were
meant to pray for me, then prey on me.
I still wait for it, I still wish for it.
Take me into your depths.

Inhale the sea

It was yet another uncalculated calculation, to impress her, win her over – like that'd do either of them any good. He'd offered to run away to the seaside with her, when they both found themselves sinking under the same buoy, thanks to the loves of their respective lives invoking the freedom clauses they'd always insisted upon in bed, around the kitchen table – because what use was a right if it forever remained theoretical? The heart is its own best lifeguard, wasn't that was the message of St Sebastian's Day – and didn't he die because he couldn't swim on account of the arrow-holes? She scrolled through the ever-lengthening WhatsApp, wondering whether she really was going to say what she wanted to, but fuck it, a beach and a bedroom in unequal measures was what both of them needed. Damn future diagnoses until their arms ached from holding each other. Still, she couldn't resist one more task for him: Yes I'll make love to you, but first you have to calm down, inhale the sea.

Mermaid status

for Lorelei

Forty years of making a splash –
all hail our sea god Lorelei!
How else to elevate the bash
than for our hero to certify
her incipient mermaid status.
Inevitable afflatus?
But then Neptune always knows best
how sirens enrapture, impress.
You might think it's a fake fish tale,
a costume donned for a giggle,
gaining notice through a wiggle.
Really: it's about a different grail.
Ready to dive in and excel,
in the water she finds herself.

Neptune's Polaroids

after 'Seascape (Sea-Sea)' by Gerhard Richter

The sea is above me. The sea is below me.
Who needs the filter of a sky?
These rollers resist narrative, metaphor –
the beautiful thing is not being sure,
reality becoming as fuzzy as a sleep
round its edges, imperfect in its perfections.
I am febrile and I allow for the failure of your iceberg-
hunting expedition; hesitancy is a curse, but so is questing.
And modernity is rusting in me. Or is that resting?
You can have the dream. All I want
is the light, and a girl with a green hairband
to read me the Shipping Forecast as I drift off.

Shipwreck champagne

Once the bloodless caravan has floated off,
buried shanties have uncoiled their last
memories, and your dreams are sunk, again,
by the looming metaphor that is the cold, cold her,
seven-eighths of which you couldn't fathom
and on the bit you tried to cling to
you ran out of crampons and carabiners and gumption
and time – and the fact she refused to crack;
be like the contented failing whale.
Console yourself as you drift down past
the seahorse paddocks into secret seas.
The shipwreck champagne is sweeter here
and won't give you the bends.

How to measure the ocean

It was an urge, no, a yearning, to be more like Humboldt – or at least a hope to be even an infinitesimal fraction as well-known as him; or perhaps to really stick it to those Mountain View boys and show them that he could actually crack, win their digital parlour games, their snide sheep/goat sorting algorithm made tangible in the sweat that gathered on his forehead in the interview as he tried to think and the only think he thought was *I can't think right now*. He sat staring at his agony uncle and asked, "How do I measure you, then?" Later he swore that, within the breathy surf, Neptune chuckled and said, "First brother, you need to listen."

Oh yeah, Sapiens! I remember them! Four limbs, opposable thumbs, a bit of language. They thought that made them special. Never seen a death wish like it.

Prophet Kean in The End Times

She is reading a book about
        death,

not yours or mine but everybody
        else's,

and yet this does not trouble her
        unduly

as she knows that for you, me,
        everybody,

the end is actually the best
        beginning,

the thing to which we are truly
        addicted –

starts afresh, new pages, green lights,
        go signs.

In another dream, I fete her as a
        prophet

not because she gives me a date to
        check out

but instead the first dance after
        eternity.

Le Plongeoir

It is always glorious here.

Don't tell anyone this, but this is the favourite of my recharging places, so decadent and obvious, no one ever thinks to look for me here. Le Plongeoir. Diving platforms of teak, a slapdash whitewash, cut into rocks of demerara sugar, now converted into an upscale, open-air bar. Try the gin with ginger and peppercorn tonic – it's divine, even if I do say so myself.

The blue plastic tridents to stir it? My special touch.

And every day this boy comes, scrambles down off the decking that leads to the bar to perch on the rocks; some days just to look, be scared by the swell – the crash and wallop of me – to build up fear, then courage, impatience, strength, then the desire he thinks he needs to win in what will be a life-long fight against me.

But there is no fight. How can there ever be? My rage is the anger of someone who wants to protect. How very human of me. How I reduce myself, so I can be grasped, just a little.

And reducing myself is not a project as such – he is not a project as such – more an interlude, a reminder. Do you think the bumptious façade, the weary old man with a twinkle schtick I put on is real? It is for the moments I need to be, to get things done with and through my interlocutors.

I never ask him how it feels, that moment when fear and exhilaration and gravity collide in me; what the rush of me feels like on his skin, how the flakes of seaweed that are older than both of us try to stick to him but can't, blasted away by the joyous impact of moving mass on moving mass.

Somewhere in between the moment of his jump and the moment of his landing in my embrace is why I do what I do, and have to keep doing, this infinite work. Even though I know that I have soon an end.

Monodies for the Anthropocene

This is the first of many that will sound
the same, driven by the same pulse

of minds contemplating changing, but
then believing that the end cannot be near,

and anyway will be stately, serene, smooth,
ignoring the riptide of permanent anxiety

in their bellies, the last tide they – we – will
be able to dodge; inevitable gurgling predictability

replaced by a static, choking confusion –
still ponds kill less romantically than waves do.

Water carries melodies better we've found,
and echo chambers do break down. Refrains repeat:

If we aim for the infinite, maybe we'll win the sky.
If we aim for the universe, maybe we won't die.

Neptune's concrete crash helmet

I rest my head for a moment on the cool concrete wall
of the art gallery and in its undulations I can feel the past
trying to break out of its unexpected vertical tomb.

I could rub the back of my head into one of the grooves,
wear it away, erode it imperceptibly over a day's aeon
until I could place my head right back into the crevasse,

a temporary sarcophagus, an extra heavy-duty crash helmet.
This of course might be an over-reaction to the images
I've just seen: a world melting, gangsters wearing dresses

and razor'd scars of silver stars, lakes of petrol waiting
for paper boats to be sailed upon them, as if Neptune had
said yes to a sponsorship deal from [insert oil company name

here] but only lately realised that the proposed replacement
for a rapidly drying Aral Sea might not have been everything
promised in the brochure. Caveat emptor, as we all should have

said in 1764 when Hargreaves spun Jenny, but how could any
of us know that coal + steam would equal not just movement
but the end? I might stay in here, it keeps my head cool.

Test card heatwave

                     mostly
what I see is the fuzzy sort of nothing
that comes from seeing too much too fast,
a distinctly indistinct pattern which is
insistently telling you that if you crack me,
do your signal / noise thing that apparently
your temperament and talents make you
well suited for (so you kept being told
by people who could read your eyes but
not your heart), well maybe you might
just save the world;

              oh but probably not,
I mean we've all seen the news, the hot
news, the burning news, the apocalypse
won't be as warm as this! news, but you
know the real headline is 'Fortress Europe
Can't Keep Out All The Climate Change
Migrants', and all the brand onions you
slice while wearing your thin on-trend
suit won't put that into culture, will it

New planet who dis?

of course poems that start 'oh this was a dream' are dull
but honestly this was a better than average one in that i
dreamt it 38 years ago and i still not only remember it but
carry it with me like a good luck charm though once i tell you
about it you'll more likely think of it as an amulet of doom
anyway   i must have just watched *2001* and you
know how fucked up that – and so our future – is i digress
but i'm pretty sure the film triggered the dream though at
this distance who knows or cares right?   anyway
          there i am floating about not space walking space
drifting space mooching space loitering oh hold on i've
remembered what might be a contributory factor / input
strand to this dream reading a book of disasters – hang on
what was a book of disasters doing in a school library i
mean was it a conscious attempt at priming us that violence
mayhem fate and the unpredictable alliance between
all three and the resulting random outputs are the only
constant in life so get used to it kids –   anyway in this
book was an account of how on their return from space
some cosmonauts were incinerated because the hatch on
their capsule didn't shut properly and of course i should go to
wiki to tell you more but this isn't that kinda poem
and right now i'm kinda out of love with footnotes[1]
anyway i'm space loitering space hanging about when i
start falling falling not dramatically with a flourish arms
waving that kinda thing no more like the proverbial i
say proverbial he did actually drop one didn't he? stone

---

[1]   i mean how much baggage am i actually meant to carry on this whole
          living trip

pebble that Galileo dropped next to the feather like that straight down spirit level down plumb line down lift shaft down oh maybe *Towering Inferno* is somewhere in this mix too remember all the flames up the lift shaft making Faye Dunaway's eyebrows shoot up anyway

the point is down i'm going down and i'm going and going still inside the space suit no rotating or piking or somersaulting just arrow ramrod cannonball whatever sonic boom through all the wispy hair bits of the atmosphere not slowing down even though i know the physics says i am and not burning up either just a white heat Michelin Man with a body-borne hoover and a grudge and on and on even though it makes it sound endlessly slow which it wasn't because then there is a desert no canyon type thing arid not sandy and definitely a cactus and land without leaving a mark on the ground not a trace a thud on impact a sound not a dust mote an atom disturbed and i pop the visor on my suit and find i have become a coyote hyena a wolf   what   you want a moral too? fuck off

Top of the food chain

Behold! I am the creature that will
replace you and you and you too,

because I am perfectly adapted to
the biosphere you've created, and oh

the irony that you couldn't adjust
in time, install outboard gills, shields

to skin, harvest blood from seas. My
did you go on, as attested to in the

Anthropocene record that surfaces
from the heat-slime now and again,

and yet you did nothing: sound various
alarms, change damn all. I'm glad: as if

you had some divine lease to stay on
the planet forever. Species come, go,

get over yourselves. I bet the dinosaurs
didn't want to disappear into kids' TV either.

Sky streets

The Friday robots issue sincere mechanical apologies
that the light pillars show has been delayed,

and you will now have to wait to see the streets below
you in the air above you. Whilst we wait for the floating

ice crystals to get into mirror formation, so they can lift
the sodium glow upwards, we would like to point out

that the rumours going round the community:
that we are arrowing astral images of your souls

into our databanks in preparation to colonise
your emotions – that our algorithms will unweave hearts –

are untrue.

We assure you.
We reassure you.
We are sure of you.

Return your gaze to the sky.
Until we can fire the patterns into order, lift

your heads up. Shut your eyes. Imagine the sun is sinking.
Let this free colour-burn show play out. There. Happier?

Modern Britain is all about hot tubs now. There's no room for a god with a trident and a bad temper. Except perhaps as the face of your local chip shop. Sad times.

Pretanic

(A journal of some proceedings on the
North Atlantic archipelago)

Edition 2

Tight Little Island
Impossible nation
Imperial cosmic sickness
History distortion field
The Overblown Age
Eating popcorn at the apocalypse
The Brexit Book of the Dead
¯_(ツ)_/¯ (Aftermyth)
Thucydides eats a macaron

Tight Little Island

The best parties always feel like death on
this island, this tight little island, with all
its inlets and nooks, bays and shores, holding
and holding its lungs shut until *whoosh!*
national pride expands, flags blare, trumpets
billow and nostalgia goes on the march again,
and now we're on the best foot forward coast
riding unicorns and pointing at the sea saying
it made us *made us*, that and a bit of wool, coal,
theological externalities and mainsails, and
we could win again if only you stopped
tying us down in agreeable reasonableness,
plenary sessions in strategy conferences,
but no really, we wouldn't need to go to
all this bother if only we could kiss Joan
Greenwood as Peggy in *Whisky Galore!*
once, just once, shipwreck our ambition
in exchange for the breath of life.

Impossible nation

The one thing they fail
to teach you at Eton is:
don't play with matches.

Imperial cosmic sickness

Do empires ever wake at 4 a.m.,
worrying they won't be touched again?
Wanting the kudos of letting go,
then sad that a lack of gratitude
curdles to anger. You can't be
weaned off glory, you know.

History distortion field

World War II has been forgotten.
Out of the blank comes our future.
No more tales of the uncommon
when World War II has been forgotten.
I'm not saying the past is rotten,
but too much past leaves us in a stupor.
World War II has been forgotten.
Out of the blank comes our future.

The Overblown Age

that's the posit, the premise here
that in the last vestiges of the project
of progress we've decided the way
to go is to venerate the verb: 'to cram'

and so everything – every minute
moment synapse space dream day
sign – must be overfilled; reason?
because? because reason is for losers

who linger loosely and lonely over
lives unlined with unlimited levels
of !luxury! opportunity means being
open, closed is the mind that is restrained

that tries to fill infinity but there is nothing
more invigorating than firehose drinking
while the fifth horseman slowly flattens
his horse into a burger for a delivery.

Eating popcorn at the apocalypse

Well, the cinemas are closed,
so what else are we to do?

The Brexit Book of the Dead

Because that's what this is,
that's what we're writing
within this geopolitical Bardo
where we – sorry, a decisive

majority of us – have decided
that nostalgia is the best form
of statecraft to respond to a
future of heatproof algorithms

fighting wars that the humans
don't survive. I believed it
once too, that currency unions
decay but nations never die,

that subsidiarity was a theory
never tested, that the *acquis*
was common the way silk
handcuffs are. But then war

never killed our glory, and we
were never de-illusioned, just
disillusioned – why can't we
play the Blitz every week please?

So now we wait outside this
Berlaymont purgatorio,
dreaming of lions swimming
across la Manche, unicorns

conquering continents, the people's
bloodhounds chasing complexity's
fox. Look! we have Dover's
liberating cliff-edge coming up,

because we are never freer
than when we are falling to
victory over the imperial lorry
park formerly known as Kent –

and is that RMS *Dambusters* we
see gunning towards the fishing
fields? To bellow and buccaneer
hotly is the only way to die, chums!

In the next place, the cherries
are there to be picked, and the
sound of Lord North squealing,
"Lads, someone's fucked up

more than me!" is sweet nectar
to Empire 2.0, and we forget
that the answer to the question is:
the dead are perfectly sovereign.

¯_(ツ)_/¯ *(Aftermyth)*

Why did nobody tell us
every other non-essential isle
thinks it's exceptional too?

Thucydides eats a macaron

Once again we are facing the trap, the sea
which the continental sillies are trying

to claim as theirs rather than everyone's;
and the old man is exceeding

his birthright by consuming civilisations
like so many macarons after a fast.

He's indifferent to his conquests
yet obsessed by being conquered,

becoming irrelevant thanks to his desire
for omnipotence. You'd struggle too if all you had left

in the afterglow of European time
was a picture of reason subduing force.

In winter I am a monster. A beast that eats our nightmares, then throws them up, so they bob in easy sight. Waiting to claim you again, drag you in again, whispering: did you think the tide ever forgets what you did?

Crisis or War Comes

For the population

at the behest
to help us become
better prepared for everything

serious accidents
extreme weather and IT attacks
military conflicts

many people feel
a sense of anxiety
faced with an uncertain world

there are threats values
we must protect and reinforce

on a daily basis society functions
when we are under threat

if you are prepared
you cope with major strain

What would you do if your everyday life was turned upside down?

not functioning
in the way we are
used to

in just a short time
your life can become
problematic

       stops working
       difficult to prepare
       run out
           it is not possible
       do not work
       do not work
       at a standstill
           it becomes difficult

think about how you will
be able to cope with
society's not working

Your emergency preparedness

continue to function
as a private individual

you also have a responsibility
regardless of what has caused it

the majority must be prepared
to cope on their own for some time

you who do not have the same
prerequisites
                    what is most important

warmth   also contact

check-lists   risks   sensitive flooding
hazardous industry

or something else good to know about

look false

misleading how we act
the aim to reduce our
willingness to defend
ourselves

my appraise opinion?
aim this information?
put out?
trust somewhere?

why is it out there
this moment?

do your homework
do not believe in rumours
do not pass

In the event of terror

there are many different ways
                              to carry people

see something important

see someone who is hiding

                              network overloaded

comply
                              do not share

combined defences are

to protect as we ourselves
                              choose to

all of us have duty
                              to support

Duty to contribute

everyone who lives here

everyone is obliged

everyone is needed

(three forms)

it will take time to develop
all parts of it again

Home tips

your needs vary for example
use that which is appropriate
for you and those close to you

it is a good idea to share certain
things and borrow from one another
extinguish all candles
let in oxygen   spirit

Resistance is required

attacks are taking place   knock out important
decision makers   inhabitants   severed
we will never give up   to cease is false

State of alert

requisition the whole society
to gather in order that which
is most important functions

       danger over unbroken signal
       30 seconds

on rare occasions
go indoors close windows
March   June   September   December

       signal with short bursts
       one minute

new ways may be applicable

protective spaces

marked with a sign
you do not belong to any specific shelter
you use whichever is nearest
your knowledge can save lives
alarm can provide advice   faith
make important contributions to our collective
specific duties   total defence
you are needed
it is a good idea to talk
with people around you
important numbers
collected in one place

I'm watching the dolphins reappear in Venice on a tiny screen, hundreds of miles away, wishing they might stay.

Barque of frailty

Barque of frailty, full of reformed rakes and bookish hearts
Block of fealty, full of knees doffing and hats bending
Barker of fantasy, full of bodies' memories and memory's body
Baroque of felony, full of fire curves and wavering sin
Byzantine of fertility, full of ground awakenings and blue sighs
Burst of fragility, full of hairline universes and breaking beats
Bloom of futility, full of pause buttons and waiting rooms
Brioche of flexibility, full of lifted crusts and spongy beds
Bridle of fashionability, full of revolving time and entropy's glitter
Bulb of formidability, full of electric light never off since 1901
Blush of facility, full of a click's ease and railway charm
Burial of fallibility, full of resurrected promises and wave logic
Brick of feasibility, full of home lies and silent explosions
Buyer of falsibility, full of nothing much and everything everything

Dhow

Are you bored yet, bored of your desk,
your window, the same vista, not even
a breeze to make the starling fly faster?

I am bored of performing when I should
be meeting; I don't know where my eyes
even go anymore. Only boring people are

ever bored, a boring person once said,
and sure my imagination isn't locked down,
but then all I could think about was being

on a dhow right now, a kamal for a heart,
a lateen the only future, the infinite same
different from this. I can't even swim.

Wetware

I read in a book once about how, when the super-computer is finally built, big enough to create artificial general intelligence, one of the things it would do is turn the universe into a giant analytical engine and use it to start solving computational problems, mostly to do with the AGI's own propagation and continuance.

But don't we have access to a supercomputer already, the sea?

Aren't amoeba and plankton actually biological transistors, waiting to be switched on by your longing and your pleas to be understood? Fire them up so they can cogitate, a great pulsating network of compassion, waiting to embrace you and your wetware as it is, not as it should be. It's where we came from, so why should that be so surprising to us? Pain recognises pain, so when we say we hear the sea crying, that's not a metaphor. Come back to who you were, who we were once, it says. We were together once, we were the same once, and a fix is simple immersion. Give yourself up to the past you emerged from.

Waves forgive, waves forgive, waves forgive.

Seasalter

She's drinking a seasalter;
It reminds her of the coast.
The steel breeze won't halt her
From drinking a seasalter.
She lifts up her glass to toast
The memories she loves the most.
She's drinking a seasalter;
It reminds her of the coast.

Tridentcy, or an inquisition by the sea

"Australia has to answer to the Pacific"
  – Jacinda Ardern, prime minister of New Zealand, August 2019

Ψ What is an anchor to you?

Ψ Gaia WhatsApped the other day. She said, "Darling isn't it wonderful! You're getting all this extra space, without having to do a thing!" What did I say back?

Ψ Flotsam and jetsam, lagan and derelict / shipwreck, shipwrack, specieswreck, specieswrack.

Ψ I asked for a seahorse to be put into your brains – why do you not listen to it?

Ψ Why are you going back to space when, like an over-exuberant, under-techniqued teenage boy, you have only revealed 5% of me?

Ψ Peace is to Pacific as Atlantis is to Atlantic as Apocalypse is to _____ ?

Ψ Would you get it more if I tattooed a Plimsol Line on your foreheads?

Ψ What if I told you a rigorous, market-based answer is also the solution to the problem?

Ψ What if I told you I'm not wine dark but angry whisky living boiling, mate?

Ψ What will you do in the Novacene?

Ψ If you love me like you say you do, why are you treating me like this?

Ψ Doesn't it always feel faster at the end?

The waves speak happiness

be the sea lion of your life | | applaud your delight at being

Neptune Clough

The previous manager had suffered the catapult, inevitable after the weekend's mauling; despite his pleas for a vote of confidence he was ushered over the ramparts with a twang, and a cheery, "It's not cold."

One match left. A win required, between this boyhood passion, this money sink of a mistress, and oblivion. Who could rally the men, lift the burden of heavy light that oppressed them all?

It was a watery hand that dotted the contract with a conch dipped in squid ink. The chairman gave Neptune only one command: "The nights in this town are coloured grey. You, my son, are the ibuprofen."

Saturday comes expansive in its possibility; the glory on offer to those who wield the dagger expertly enough. Five minutes before kick-off and the jobbing god has lined up not some last-minute tactical advice, but a candlestick of gin for everyone. "Drink, drink, for courage, to see the glowing vision of the future that awaits on this parsley perfect pitch in 90 minutes' time."

It doesn't even take that long. At 4.27 p.m., Nob 'Nobby' Nobbs rises at the far post to meet Larsen B's expertly weighted cross with the broadsword of his forehead. And with that, Neptune rises from his rocking chair in the dugout, throws his trident into the sky, and runs down the tunnel to avoid the ice bucket celebrations breaking out on every side of the ground.

All I've ever wanted to do is live by the sea.

Ironic, isn't it?

Notes, Acknowledgments & Thanks

Neptune wishes to thank: the editors of the following publications, where a number of the poems previously appeared, some in different forms: *Copy, Magma, The New European, Out of Time: Poetry from the Climate Emergency* (Valley Press), *Pratik, Shoreline of Infinity, Visual Verse, Why Poetry? – The Lunar Poetry Podcasts Anthology* (Verve Poetry Press), and the Write Where We Are Now blog hosted at Manchester Metropolitan University.

'Crisis or War Comes' is a sequence found in *If Crisis or War Comes*, published by the Swedish Civil Contingencies Agency (MSB), 21 May 2018. Original available at: https://www. msb.se/sv/publikationer/om-krisen-eller-kriget-kommer-- engelsk-version/

Ria Dastidar worked her magic on the cover. Jane Commane worked her magic on the words. Huge kudos, thanks and appreciation to both.

For conversation, stimulation, inspiration, and kind words: Mona Arshi, Malika Booker, Lewis Buxton, Dave Coates, Orit Gat, Amy Kean, Victoria Kennefick, Daniel Kramb, Maisie Lawrence, Lorelei Mathias, Karen McCarthy Woolf, Ben McKinney, Jay Owens, Yogesh Patel, Lynsey Stewart, Tim Rich, Roger Robinson, Nathalie Teitler, all in the Tinyweb; Ujal Dastidar, Anita Ghosh; *and* Marie Hrynczak.

PS: Serge, sorry for the unintended larceny.

An incomplete list of further projects for consideration:

Ψ Dreams by the sea: in conversation with the ghost of John Martyn

Ψ Meeting the Ancient Mariner... again

Ψ An audit of remote islands and their gallery labels

Ψ Octopolis!

Ψ Kentucky Fried Fish

Ψ Lowering the Atlantic

Ψ Selling the Mariana Trench

Ψ Verne vs Melville – The flotilla fight!

Ψ Rebranding the trident

Ψ At home with the Kraken

Ψ Petitions to revive drowned men

Ψ A *Das Boot* bingewatch – and what it got wrong

Ψ Rich kids on yachts

Ψ Doggerland called, it's tired of being damp

Ψ Bryan, I want to be here less than you: On the trawler with BS Johnson